MEMORY MAP

poems by

Tara Prakash

Finishing Line Press
Georgetown, Kentucky

MEMORY MAP

ACKNOWLEDGMENTS

To my grandparents (Dadi, Dada, Nani, and Nana)—thank you for a childhood full
of treasured moments. For every shared laugh, story, and meal. How lucky I was to
grow up with you.

Publisher: Leah Huete de Maines
Editor: Christen Kincaid
Cover Art: Hale Woodruff
Author Photo: Hamza Bakkach
Cover Design: Elizabeth Maines McCleavy

Order online: www.finishinglinepress.com
also available on amazon.com

Author inquiries and mail orders:
Finishing Line Press
PO Box 1626
Georgetown, Kentucky 40324
USA

Contents

I REMEMBER PEOPLE

Dear Nani

I'm writing to you from a mountain top. You always love reading my pieces, so I'm sending you a few stories with this letter. I've enlarged the font, so you can read them. I know you're forgetting so much, so let me tell you what I remember.

I remember bowls of Annie's mac-and-cheese with peas and purified water from a pitcher. I loved that mac-and-cheese, and I also loved the bowls. You always used the same one, ceramic white and laced with green tulips on the lip. One time, I asked my mom to make the mac-and-cheese, just the way you did, but it didn't taste quite the same. When I asked why the water was purified, not the normal water I had at home, you said "Only the best for my favorite granddaughter!" I remember smiling.

Even when Nana spent hours in his room, lying on the gray comforter and staring at the chipped ceiling with glazed eyes, you were moving around, grabbing balled up socks and playing cards trapped under the legs of kitchen chairs, bony fingers hammering nails into the wall to hang up my school pictures and family photos, light bouncing off smiling faces.

I remember watching Young Sheldon in your living room in the evenings. Usually for the first twenty minutes of each episode, you would be bustling around in the small kitchen, pulling out chocolate-almond Dove bars and pouring us glasses of fizzing Coke, but I loved when you would join Rahul and me on the couch, the embroidered burgundy blanket draped across our laps. I'm pretty sure I looked at you more than the television screen, how a smile broke across your face whenever Missy and Sheldon teased each other, reminded you of me and Rahul, I think. You were so pretty when you laughed, your head thrown back, slightly crooked smile and dimpled cheeks, dark eyes creased. I don't remember you ever scolding us, even when bits of chocolate broke off the bar and fell onto the carpet, lost in the plush crimson. I always fell asleep before the episode ended, my soft snore pushing into the quiet room.

I wrote this piece based on an "I remember" prompt I gave myself curled up by the bed. It's a generic prompt, an easy one. But I couldn't wait to jump in, to close my eyes and picture your egg-shell white plaster walls, your large fluorescent light bulbs, the small, manicured lawn out front. I do a lot with memory in my writing. It's funny how memory works, how I can remember which photos are taped on your fridge but lying in bed some nights, staring up at the glowing stars taped on my ceiling, I forget the sound of your

1

laugh. I have a bit of an obsession with memory in my writing, maybe because there's so much of it. There's always more to remember. And I'm watching you and learning how easy it is to forget.

I remember you would carry me to the bed, your fingers pressing gently into my ribs, until you no longer picked me up. I learned this one evening as I lay sprawled on the couch, my brother's voice muted. I waited for you to scoop me up, for your cool hands on my waist, but instead you gently shook my leg and told me I was too heavy for you to lift. When I looked up at you, lines creased your cheeks, your dimples. I went to my red-and-white trundle bed that night with a lump in my throat and fell asleep to Rahul's voice talking on the phone in the room next to mine, where he slept. I woke up in the morning to find clumps of dark brown hair in the bathroom trash can, thick locks among cherry Dum-Dum wrappers and Old Navy t-shirt receipts. That was how I found out. I ran, crying, to the kitchen, where I found you. You set down your whisk and pushed the bowl of egg yolks to the side to sit down with me, groaning as you lowered yourself onto the cool linoleum tiles. Our backs against the refrigerator, you pressed your hand firmly onto mine. Later that afternoon, I curled up in the sagging bean bag in the corner of the room, my face in the fuzz. When you survived the chemotherapy, and the doctors removed the lump in your breast, I thought you were immortal. Then aging kicked in. I could see every day that you weren't.

I remember Wii tennis, standing on the crimson carpet, flinging the remote around to hit the ball flying toward us on the screen. We almost hit each other so many times, a light breeze from a remote whizzing too close to skin. I got a bruise from when I slammed my arm mid-swing into the side of the brown sectional couch. You were never too good at playing. You'd have to sit down on the couch a few points into the game, out of breath, your shoulders pressed against the fabric back of the couch, and you'd lose some leverage on your swing. So, I played easy on you. Some points, I even pretended to not see the ball and swung a few seconds too late. You would always grin when you won, spinning around on the carpet, your arms flying around your waist in celebration.

When we hung out yesterday, my friend told me to remove some of the details. They're unnecessary, she said. I nodded, smiled politely. I didn't know how to tell her that the kitchen isn't just bright, but sunlight falls through the window in showers. The carpet isn't red; it is maroon with flecks of gold and auburn if you kneel down and stare at it long enough. The speakers aren't low quality; the voices crackle like static into the family room. Here is me: a girl with an attachment to detail. The carpet is not red.

Whenever I walked to the bathroom, I would stop at the portrait of your brother, clean-shaven face, dimpled cheeks, military uniform ironed and smooth. He died in a plane, you had told me once, after I'd asked a few times. When I probed further, you suggested a game of carrom and walked out of the room before I could respond. I have a lot of questions. What did you want to be or do in your life? Did you get it? Were you loved in the way you wanted to be?

I remember tea-stained photographs slid into vermillion photo albums, your plump figure standing on the roof of your uncle's apartment flat, your smiling face fading from the page. You had long hair, reaching down to the small of your back, your aquamarine sari losing color. In these photos, the sun was behind you, yellows and oranges splashed across a smoggy sky. Kneeling on the carpet staring at these images, I imagined standing there with you, the India heat hugging us. In later photos, farther into the album, I could see you and Nana, cradling crying babies in your arms, my mom and my uncle. The two of you were sitting on a purple couch. It must have been soon after you moved to the United States. I noticed after looking at the photo closer that your smile didn't quite reach your eyes, your cheeks weren't dimpled. Did you want to move? Were you happy? I wish we talked about me less.

I'm not doing you justice. In a few days, I'll share this again with my friend, and she'll smile and tell me she thinks you are the sweetest grandmother ever. I will sigh when she's not looking. The time when you ran through the house slapping Rahul with a ping-pong racket because he let the pancakes burn will run through my mind. You are not sweet. "Sweet" is for grandmothers who sit at the kitchen table on Sunday afternoons and knit green and white scarves while drinking chamomile tea with cinnamon biscuits.

I remember swimming at the community pool near your house, how you groaned as you moved into the water, your legs aching and sore. Later, you didn't go in at all. You just sat on the reclining pale green chairs on the deck, your bare feet resting on the slabs of concrete baking under the sun. You used to play catch with us at the pool, a transparent red ball soaring between our pruned and wrinkled hands, but later, only Rahul and I played. It was never as fun. Sometimes, we would toss the ball to you, underhand and light, and you could usually catch it, and throw it limply back. But most of the time, you just lay on the chair's webbed surface, eyes closed, wrinkled hands folded on top of your stomach.

I'm trying to do more creative nonfiction writing, so I'm writing about you. I think what I'm writing will make you sad, so I won't share it with you. You're forgetting things, like my age and how to make instant coffee in the mornings and where you've put your cane when you use the bathroom after lunch. I'm writing these memories down because when I found this prompt, you came to my mind first.

Red I

Tiger's blood,
I say. I'm six, and I'm ordering shaved
ice from the Clay Boys stand
in Bethesda Row down the street
from my house. I like the ferocity
and feist

of the syllables. In a few
moments, the tall boy with the stained apron hands
me the cone. Deep red
is seeped across the ice.
I bite off a piece before my mom
hands him the three dollar bills.

Cherry spills into my mouth.

Handfuls

I pick blueberries the same way I hold my grandmother's
hand as we walk across the asphalt parking lot to Benihana's,
Pressing gently, testing the strength of peeling blue skin.

There are many ways to love a person and only some will break them down,
like my grandfather, who knows me in sneezes,
knows me in the contours of my shoulders,

pictures my six-year-old self licking a lemon popsicle on the hot stone
bench outside Brookside gardens, a day before he went in for the surgery
that left him blind, feeling our hair for height when we visit.
At mealtimes, his plate is a clock.

My father spoons fried rice at three o'clock
and red vegetable curry at eleven o'clock,
and as I sit across the table and watch him, I wonder if he is okay, my father,
who cried for the first time that day
when he left the hospital,

me upstairs, throwing
a rubber ball into a hoop fitted onto the frame
of my bunk bed, that was how he found me, and that was where I learned

that tugging on the hem of a crying man's
navy T-shirt, asking "What's happening?"
only makes him cry harder.

A frail hand, blueberries spilling, a melting lemon popsicle.
An unraveling navy T-shirt.
I cup my hands and despair that they cannot hold more.

I REMEMBER OUR MOTHER EARTH

On Erosion

I bend down to kiss the grass and call it prayer.
My jeans smudge with dirt at the kneecaps. Behind me,
the swing set groans with age.
I say *I love this place* out loud, how
sprawled out here, I can feel the world's soily belly
breathe alongside mine. The fat red-white woodpecker

At the edge of the field beats bark into heartbeat, lined up with my own.
I don't think I am any different from this place. The cloud above me
looks like the dome of a button mushroom, a large curved puff of white.
Maybe when I am old

And lying on my bed beneath a cardinal red comforter,
and my chest feels filled with sticky
sap, and my voice croaks like a yellow-bellied bullfrog by the lakeside,
I will wake up and the blue river veins in my hand will be pressed
into smooth brown skin again and I will be sprawled out here on the grass,

inhaling honeysuckle, and wind will brush away my hair like a mother's
hand. Maybe right now, if I ask for rain, the clouds will break open
like the leaves hugging the arm of the willow pinned to the edge
of my childhood playground, where years ago I climbed high enough
to let the sun hit my throat, where I held the branch and leaned forward, my
sweaty palms pressed against the coarse skin, the bark-covered
body holding me like a promise, where I swung toward the ground,

Where I dropped to soft soil and ran, my small body tumbling
into tall grass, where I stopped, crouched,
to let my footsteps catch up to me,
my shadow stretched by afternoon sun, my breath stumbling into breeze.

Wind breaks the mushroom-shaped cloud
above me into wispy strands of white.
The sky spins and the crescent moon moves with it.
Supple bodies always crack with age. River erodes rock.
This is how the world is.

I close my eyes and wait for the sky to come
to a gentle stop. Tears wash down my sandstone cheeks,
but everything around me is dry.

Our Star, A Sestina

8.3 minutes, and its light reaches us. When we look at the sky
We are looking into the past.
The sky is a map of history. I look up into the dark sea glass above
Me. I can't help but wonder if you are one of those pinpricks of light
Pulsing, twinkling at me. I wish I could've told you I loved you, Grandfather,
      but time
Rivered wrinkles into your body, scarred your memory

With the art of forgetting, recollections of sand scattering through your
      memory,
Just as starlight dozes in the early morning sky.
Those three words wouldn't mean anything to you. If I could, I would send
      the past
Up to you on a wisp of cloud, of good-night stories, playing in the waves,
      summer evenings bathed in firefly light,
So I wouldn't have to look into the ashy charcoal above

To find you, I could have been lying in your sunburnt arms, my head against
      your cotton blue shirt, and we'd be looking above
Together, and instead of me searching for the distant beacon of your
      memory,
We would simply be staring at the droplets of grieving light
Treading water in that deep oceanic sky,
And we could fall back in grass tipped with dew and forget the past.
There wouldn't be any fog of regret, of time

Playing tricks on us. We could pretend that time
Was only a game, that no one would ever have to live above.
But now the only time I can be in your arms is in the past,
So I walk through the ivy snaked pathway of memory.
I don't want years to rob you from my mind, but the sky
Is a living, breathing example of what happens when sunlight

Rises, washing away all the starlight,
From its short existence. I wish you wouldn't fade each time
A new day begins, each time the sky
Drains its blue-black tub. Even though you've dwindled from above,
Not even the strongest sun could steal you from our hearts, our memory.
You will always be part of our past,

And we will never forget you. You're in the sky's past.
You're part of the sky and you're part of the earth and now we have enough
        light

To do anything. I hope moving on is not betrayal, for every night I go
        outside and look for you. You will never leave my memory.
I find you, find your smiling eyes in the twilight. Time
Does not apply to the stars. Those punctures of light will forever be in the
        darkness above.
All I need to do to remember you is look up at the sky.

It takes 8.3 minutes for our star's light
To reach me. Looking up, I glimpse ping-pong matches, late movie nights,
strawberry picking in the heat of summer.
An entire story unfolding in the sky.

And that's all I need to remember you, Grandfather. The past.

Red II

Matadors
used red capes not to attract
the attention of the bulls they fight.
But to hide their bloodstains.

Red is the first color babies can see,
Maybe the chapped lips of a mother.
It's the first color to fade from evening
sunsets. Red is the least common color
of sea glass, which is probably why
the jars on my bookshelf are filled
with greens and blues and a few browns.

Rarely does red make an appearance in nature. It's

too bright,
too brash,
too loud.

Try camouflaging against leaves
and you would be killed immediately. Red
can't hide, even if it tries.

It's everywhere.

This, Too, is Prayer

The hills are stiff with age, and wind breathes into the grass, and we watch from the bridge. Above us, moths swarm like butterflies. In this place teeming with life, he looks less like he is my dying grandfather and more like a boy tired from the Superman roller coaster at Six Flags. The nursing home down the road watches us, a concrete balcony above a gaping grin of smudged window. The place is called Sunrise, which is odd, because isn't it the end? His eyes close. He lets his long bony hands, piano hands, slip onto his lap, blue veins like rivers beneath his skin. The wind blows his shirt up into a potbelly. A moth lands on his elbow, the hard point where his bone stretches his flesh, and he flinches—like the moth's body has climbed its way to the decay. Tiny things can do that. He smiles, a half crescent that dimples his cheeks. "Outside is sacred," he once told me when he came over for lunch, as I was cleaning the mahogany dining table of stained napkins and plastic forks. It was the most he'd said to me all evening. Even after he lumbered to the bathroom down the hall, his breath stuck in the air, heavy with bourbon and cigarettes. Now, the moth walks around his knee, tiny legs exploring his brown skin, bark. I watch him, his faded eyes blank like an early morning sky or something late—so much later. He bends down, stilted movements. His lips move like a kiss—I learn watching him that this is how to cherish something. Rain falls inside this temple like a promise. The moth is still on his knee. He is whispering—this old, old man in a wheelchair on a bridge. A raindrop lands on my bottom lip. I lick it up and swallow it down

> My throat, into my
> Belly, thinking about how
> This, too, is prayer.

I REMEMBER GRIEF, MEMORY, A BRAIN SCAN, PAIN, FRIENDSHIP, DIRECTION, TIME

The Girl Who Birthed a Moon

It came out of her quickly, a heavy, gray being pushed out of her thick walls. It was dark, rough, sharp in places, and she howled as it left her body. When the doctors looked at her ultrasound and told her it was a moon she was birthing, not a little boy or girl, she thought a bundle of light would come out. She forgot that without the sun, the moon was just a plain gray rock orbiting Earth. She lay in her hospital bed, weakened, in the days that followed the birth, taking two showers a day where she washed the torn, red skin of her core in lukewarm water. She was sent home a week later, her moon safely buckled into his car seat in the back of their camouflage green Toyota. At every stop sign, she would look at him through the smudged rearview mirror, chuckle at the taut seat buckles pulled over his chubby, rotund body. She learns to wear long sleeves so his sharp edges don't puncture the skin of her forearms, that the third page of *Goodnight Moon* is his favorite, that there is only one section, the extra-large kids, where she can find clothes for him at Nordstrom's. After they read each night, she presses her chapped lips gently to his craters and crevices. "Goodnight, moon," she whispers, and counts down the hours until morning when she can scoop him up again. She teaches herself to ignore the looks, the whispers and giggles as she lathers sunscreen onto his gray body and then pushes him down the electric red slide at the local playground. Julia's mother, Atrice, visits a month later, drives up in a bright blue Honda to the green bungalow. She is thrilled by her grandson, claps her veiny, pale hands as he rolls down the soft carpet towards her. The sagging skin of her forearms bleed when she hugs him, but Julia tells her where the band aids are: on the chestnut table in the front hall, for easy access. Moon sits there, in his extra-large highchair with his Adidas shorts and electric blue shirt squeezed around his round body, silently watching his mother slice the knife into a thick watermelon core, the flies swarming the fruit basket. Later in the year, moon stops rolling out of bed. He spends the day in his room, his craters pressed against the blue sheets. When moon doesn't get out of bed for four days straight, Julia calls a family friend, a doctor, worried, says her son is chained to the bed, perhaps by depression or anxiety. The doctor tells her he'll be right over and asks her how many miscarriages she's had. She begs the doctor to leave, shoving curling green bills towards him for the visit and pushing him towards the door. She sobs as he leaves, throwing her body over her moon. She isn't wearing long sleeves or gloves, and the skin on her forearms and hands bleed, rivulets of red down his cratered body.

//

████████████████ a heavy, gray ████████████████
████ she was birthing, not ████████████ a bundle of light ████
████ She ████████████ washed the torn, red ███ of her core in
lukewarm water. ████████████████████ She learns to wear
sleeves ████████████████████████████████████, that the
third ██ Goodnight, ████ is his favorite. ████████ each night, she
presses her chapped lips ████ to his ████████ crevices.
████████ she whispers, and counts ████ the hours. She teaches ████
████████████ him ████ the ███ playground. Julia's mother, ████
visits █████. She ████████ claps ████████████ as he rolls ████
████████████ towards her. ████████████ her ███ arms bleed when
she hugs him, ████████████████ the band aids are: on the ████
table. ████████████ easy access. Moon sits ████████████
████████ with ██ Adidas shorts ████████ squeezed around his ████
body, ████ watching ██ mother ████ knife into a ████ watermelon
core, ██ flies swarming ████████████. Later ████████ moon stops
rolling out of bed. ████████ Julia calls ████████████ a doctor, ████████
███ says her son is chained ████████ by depression or anxiety.
The doctor ████████████████████ asks ███ how many miscarriages
████████ She begs ████████ him ████████████████████
towards the door. ████████ She sobs, ████████ throwing her body over
her moon. ████████████████████ her forearms ████████
bleed, ████████ red ████████████

//

████████ a ████ gray ███ birthing, ████████ She ████████
████ learns ██ whispers ████ teaches ██ him, ██ her██
████████ body, her moon ████ red ████████

Red III

Red ranges from scarlets
to crimsons. It has historically
been associated with sacrifice,

danger, and courage. Modern
surveys in Europe and the United States
show red to be associated with heat,
passion, anger, sexuality, love,
and joy. In China and India,
it is the color symbolizing
happiness and good fortune.
Red speeds up our heart rate,
blood flow, temperature. It seems like red

is everything.

I Run into Memory in the Ice Cream Aisle at Whole Foods

I've never talked to her before, but I've seen her
around town, so I know what she looks like. She is standing
in front of the freezer doors,
drawing circles in the fog on the glass.

She is short, built like an hourglass,
a heavy-set base and slim middle. I watch her
stand on the tiptoes of her
Converse sneakers to reach
the pint of Rocky Road ice
cream on the highest metal shelf.

She looks at me, "Hi, Lia." I'm surprised
she knows my name, but then I'm not. Her face dimples,
and her dark eyes sparkle. We walk up together to the cash
register, her trailing slightly behind. She follows me to the sliding
Doors after printing out her receipt.

We reach her car, a blue Toyota
mini parked at the far end of the lot.
She pops open the trunk
and drops her bag in. I hear the grenadine
glass clank against other items.

Memory checks the silver watch wrapped
around her plump wrist. I notice the hands
are spinning counter-

clockwise. She tells me she has time,
offers to see my father at the local nursing home,
help him remember things.

We don't talk as we drive. She plugs her phone
into the Apple Carplay and plays a song on low
volume, tells me it was one of my mom's favorites
when I was young. As I weave through the traffic,
I listen carefully to the lyrics trickling through the static.

When we enter the room, my father is on the couch
watching a tennis match, except his eyes don't follow the ball
as it flies from one side to the other. He's just staring
right at the net, where nothing really happens.
Something pulls in my chest as the door shuts behind me.

Memory makes herself at home.
She slips off her boots and drops her jacket on the ground,
sprawls on the couch beside him, her feet almost touching his thighs.
I try to squeeze next to her on the couch, but she takes up all the space
on the cushions, so I sit in front of them on the carpet.

Memory tells him he's always been good at tennis. Her voice is loud
in this room.

He blinks twice, quickly.

She sits up and scooches closer to him, places a hand on his skin,
Tells him about his trashman job in high school, how he couldn't
Be a kid. The way she talks, it's like someone has died.

He nods, but his eyes look shiny. She stands up from the couch,
walks to the mahogany wood cabinet
beside the television and pulls it open.
She sifts through and takes out a homemade
card I drew him for his ninetieth birthday.

She tells him about the poems he wrote for his sister, things about light
and her smile, how her eyes would open wide, so wide, when
she started to tell a story.

I smile. To remember again. But his cheeks are wet. I whisper
To memory to ease off, but she is already striding to the metal
refrigerator. She pulls open the door, silver and bare,
takes out a Tupperware container of frozen mac-and-cheese,
Tells him this is what their mother made on pay day with fresh cheddar.

He sounds strangled, the way he sobs.
I swallow hard. To remember again.
I tell Memory to go, that she's cruel, ruthless.

She looks hurt.
She takes her time sliding her feet
into her boots, slipping her jacket on.
When she leaves, the door slams shut behind her,

echoing through the walls for long after.

The brain scan of the mouse I'm studying at my internship

Shows the way the microglia hugs the neuron, makes today
Into memory. I change the color to red, tracing the branches
With my cursor, wonder where the roots go, what the body
Remembers.

It's hard to think this matters. This is a mouse, something
With a memory of cheese and cat.

I want to know what is in my grandfather's brain,
Like when he stares at me for seconds too long,
If it is the microglia to blame,
If it's not hugging the neuron right,
If it's suffocation happening. Sometimes, too much
Love can kill something.

This is how I learn of forgetfulness,
When someone teaches themself
To leave something behind.

I flip through the scans, the microglia distancing
From the neuron, the red farther and farther,
Like animation. This is how you watch
A memory fall apart. How do you hold a microglia close?

What I mean is, this is scary, the way this movie
Is playing and I keep clicking through the scans,
One by one by one. The microglia is moving, farther
And farther, and the mouse keeps forgetting,

And on the screen, it is my grandfather I see,
Creased eyes empty, chapped lips
Mouthing something that sounds like one thing and then another,
And I flip back to the first slide of the mouse brain, where the microglia
Hugs the neuron, so close and tight, like it will never let go,
And I stare and stare and let tears blur my vision
Until the neuron and the microglia are

one.

Red IV

Only 1-2% of the world's population
has red hair. Redheads are more sensitive
to sunlight, and their hair is more resistant
to turning

gray with age.

I learn in Dr. Schropfer's first period
accelerated biology class that leukemia
is the result of an abnormal and excessive
production of blood cells. They keep multiplying
and can stop healthy blood cells
from working properly.

Red is destructive.
It can't be controlled.
It has a way of defying time.

At the same time, it is weak.

T in *Tetris*

I took your sweatshirt from your suitcase, we bought
it at Target together on a rainy Tuesday, it's turquoise with loose threads
and a torn tag. The electric yellow "for sale" sign on the house you moved
into, your baby blue Toyota pulling up to the curb one rainy afternoon,

I watched you jump on the trampoline in your front lawn,
pressed my fingers against the window glass until you caught my eye
And waved for me to join you. It was thundering, torrential rains, but we
flipped and jumped and played popcorn until we were soaked to the heart.

We unloaded your car together, fit the contents of your trunk into your
townhome, my townhome too for the amount of time
I spent there in the years to come, the T in tetris, the blocks trapped beneath
each other like words below my tongue,
until they unraveled, and it was suddenly an easy game to talk to you.

I travel to the airport, touch my
nose to the glass and watch the runway,
try to find you in the tiny airplane window. You take off
Before I can, I cry to myself as I pour tablespoon

upon tablespoon of turmeric, tarragon,
thyme into a plastic mixing bowl. *More thyme,
more thyme, more time*, I moan
as I shake the spice bottle, I thrust

it into the oven to the ticking clock, Mother tries the teacake,
spits it into the sink basin, tells me she tastes tears
in the batter. I sit on the carpet, swaddle myself in your sweatshirt,
your pungent peppermint scent,

Laundry detergent steals you the next afternoon when I go back and
smell the Tide honeysuckle lavender, you wait three rings
before you pick up the telephone today, your voice pierced with static,
you talk with thorns stuck in the space between your teeth.

I threw out your sweatshirt today, tossed it in the trash can
For Goodwill, your trousers, too, and your teddy bear, I'm calling you
As they lie on the curb next to the broken tree, the truck
will come soon to carry them away, the T in treasure, the broken button-
eyes, the turned-down Magic Marker mouth, no,

I'll bring them inside with me, cradle them in the crook of my elbow,
set them on the table as I eat my three-pm snack, it's tangy, stings
my tonsils, the tamarind and turmeric, no,
it's the thyme, too much thyme, too much time

Without you.

Red V

Of all the colors, I see red
the most. The fiery spill across the sky during soccer practice
Each 8pm Tuesday in the summer, the blood streaked on my skin,
a part of me inside my body now
outside of it. When I stare at a scab,

It feels like a discarded cigarette, ashy and pushed
Into the soil like a hug, like a suffocation,
Moments from sparking a wildfire across
All the pine trees in front of me and my gray-white home

And the people inside of it,
And all else I love.

They say red is rare in nature.
But they're wrong.

It is everywhere, if you look.

Memory Map

Where are we going? she will ask. Hold her hand in yours as you cross the dim living room. Trace her veins with your thumb, rivers in a tea-stained map.

Sit with her on the dark blue couch at the corner of the room, don't wince when her bony hip juts into yours as she leans into you. It'll make her sad. There is a key on the map. If Grandma whines, take her to the restroom, the square with the rounded black figures, and then after, put her purple *Contigo* water bottle into the sliding drawer. She doesn't know when enough is enough.

If she wakes up from her afternoon nap with a smile, then she has energy. You can take her up Cannon Mountain, the jagged line in the bottom left of the page. All of these trails, full of dappled sunlight and criss-crossed roots on soft soil, end up nowhere, a barren field with browning grass and cracked earth. Be sure to pack her trail mix and her North Face fleece sweatshirt. It gets cold near the top. You probably won't get there, though. She gets tired easily. When you descend, hold her hand in yours, gently. Veins are delicate and they break easy. The river is churning, curving and wrapping around heavy rocks. Be careful when you cross.

Set her down gently on the soft eggshell comforter, let her curl up and fall asleep to the whirring heater. Rest her soft blanket on top of her, the one with pale rubber duckies bobbing on an endless expanse of bathtub water. Wake her up after 137 minutes. She might sleep forever if you stay where you are right now, sitting on the linoleum tiles outside her bedroom door, your head resting against the polished wood as you listen to her soft snores. If her stomach grumbles, bring her to a restaurant (it's the rough sketch of the fork and knife below the mountain line), and then sit with her in the vermilion booth and keep her company. Lightly place your hand on top of hers to remind her you're there. She might forget her meal order, she does sometimes. Just know she'll want the mac-and-cheese with extra peas. Her hand sometimes shakes, so if she spills her herbal tea, wipe it up quickly.

If it gets on the map, drop it into the restaurant's plastic garbage can. It's not worth it; the paper is blank anyway, and the tea will make the ink run in rivers.

Coda

Time, did it slip through my fingers, flow,
Subtly as water? My little big brother,
Running across the pastures with his yellow-red kite, where did that go?
Footsteps trailing mine, hands clasped, my mother.

I can see the time pass in the creases of my
grandfather's eyes. His skin lined with the trick of time, if only
It wouldn't go so fast, then we wouldn't need to say so many goodbyes.
All too soon, if just once, my world could live forever, we wouldn't be so lonely,

But if all worlds lasted forever,
Would new ones be born? Babies gaze at the world with big eyes, bright,
seeing things they've never seen before, the old watch with
Eyes that have seen too much, the faded red pale that follows a dark night.

Time forces us to make use of what we have, unfurled,
to say goodbye and hello to all the ever-changing worlds.

Tara Prakash is the 2025 National Youth Poet Laureate Runner-Up and the 9th Youth Poet Laureate of the United States South. She also holds the titles of inaugural Maryland Youth Poet Laureate and 2024 Montgomery County Youth Poet Laureate. A three-time National Young Arts winner and two-time Scholastic Art & Writing National Gold and Silver Medalist (as well as an American Voices Medalist), Tara has had her work recognized by the *New York Times,* Princeton University, the National Council of Teachers of English, and *Narrative Magazine.* Her work has appeared in *Best American High School Writing, Blue Marble Review,* and *The Daphne Review,* among others, and her poetry has been nominated for a Pushcart Prize. She has performed at The Kennedy Center, the National Press Club, the Smithsonian Institution, and other venues. She is the founder of the literary-arts nonprofit Write to Right, where she teaches creative writing to under-resourced youth as a tool for self-transformation. Tara is an incoming freshman at Princeton University.

www.ingramcontent.com/pod-product-compliance
Lightning Source LLC
Chambersburg PA
CBHW022056080426
42734CB00009B/1375